Let's Go Outdoors!

LET'S WALK IN THE WOODS

By Tina Benjamin

Gareth Stevens
PUBLISHING

I0808488

Please visit our website, www.garethstevens.com. For a free color catalog of all our high-quality books, call toll free 1-800-542-2595 or fax 1-877-542-2596.

Library of Congress Cataloging-in-Publication Data

Benjamin, Tina.
Let's walk in the woods / by Tina Benjamin.
p. cm. — (Let's go outdoors!)
Includes index.
ISBN 978-1-4824-2633-5 (pbk.)
ISBN 978-1-4824-2634-2 (6 pack)
ISBN 978-1-4824-2635-9 (library binding)
1. Forest animals — Juvenile literature. 2. Forest ecology — Juvenile literature. I. Benjamin, Tina. II.Title.
QH541.5.F6 B46 2016
591.73—d23

First Edition

Published in 2016 by
Gareth Stevens Publishing
111 East 14th Street, Suite 349
New York, NY 10003

Editor: Ryan Nagelhout
Designer: Samantha DeMartin

Photo credits: Cover, pp. 1, 5 oliveromg/Shutterstock.com; p. 7 Aleksey Stemmer/Shutterstock.com; p. 9 (deer) Kalinina Alisa/Shutterstock.com; p. 9 (raccoon) Debbie Steinhausser/Shutterstock.com; p. 9 (rabbit) Peter Wey/Shutterstock.com; p. 9 (woodpecker) Panu Ruangjan/Shutterstock.com; p. 11 Richard Guijt Photography/Shutterstock.com; p. 13 Menno Schaefer/Shutterstock.com; pp. 15, 24 (squirrel) Pi-Lens/Shutterstock.com; pp. 17, 19 wavebreakmedia/Shutterstock.com; p. 21 Carl Day/Shutterstock.com; p. 23 artcphotos/Shutterstock.com

Printed in the United States of America

CPSIA compliance information: Batch #CS15GS: For further information contact Gareth Stevens, New York, New York at 1-800-542-2595.

Contents

Let's take a walk!
I love to walk
in the woods.

There is a path
to walk on.
Make sure
you don't get lost!

Lots of different animals live in the woods.

I see a red fox!

It moves very fast.

Squirrels love the woods, too. They like to climb trees.

I walk with my friend Kyle.

He likes to look
for birds.

Owls live in trees.
They come out at night.

Owls love to hoot!

Words to Know

red fox

squirrel

Index